THE CONCEPT OF KHALIFA

UNVEILING THE MEANING AND MAJESTY

VOLUME 1

FARHAT NIGEEN

Apna Book Publisher: Empowering Your Self-Publishing Journey
DBA: APUBS PUBLISHING AND SERVICES OPC PVT LTD.

Contact Us
Phone: 6006373599
Email: help.apnapublish@outlook.com
Website: www.apnapublisher.in
Address: Nowgam Bypass, Srinagar, Jammu and Kashmir, 190015

Book Details
Title: The Concept of Khalifa Unveiling the Meaning and Majesty
Authors: Farhat Nigeen
ISBN: 978-93-6303-955-1
Prize: ₹ 199.00

ISBN 978-93-6303-955-1
US $ 10.00
51000 >
9 789363 039551

Dedicated to everyone who is committed to learning

Contents

بِسْمِ اللَّهِ الرَّحْمَنِ الرَّحِيمِ

Assalamualaikum Warahmatullahi Wabarakatuh. I am thankful to Allah for allowing me to write my first book about the concept of Khalifa. I pray that this work will instill feelings of love for Allah into the hearts and minds of all people, encouraging them to please the Creator.

The Quran clearly shows that Allah wanted to create a khalifa (leader) on earth. Insha Allah, this book will explain the concept of khalifa in different Volumes. This book is **Volume 1 of The Concept of Khalifa According to the Quran and Sunnah.**

Sura Baqara 2: 30

وَإِذْ قَالَ رَبُّكَ لِلْمَلَائِكَةِ إِنِّي جَاعِلٌ فِي الْأَرْضِ خَلِيفَةً ۖ قَالُوا أَتَجْعَلُ فِيهَا مَنْ يُفْسِدُ فِيهَا
وَيَسْفِكُ الدِّمَاءَ وَنَحْنُ نُسَبِّحُ بِحَمْدِكَ وَنُقَدِّسُ لَكَ ۖ قَالَ إِنِّي أَعْلَمُ مَا لَا تَعْلَمُونَ

Remember when your Lord said to the angels, "I am going to place a successive human authority on earth." They asked 'Allah', "Will You place in it someone who will spread corruption there and shed blood while we glorify Your praises and proclaim Your holiness?" Allah responded, "I know what you do not know."

The Beginning of Creation

Adam عَلَيْهِ السَّلَام created by Allah as the first human leads us to the question: Was he Allah's initial creation?

Allah says in the Quran in Sura Anbiya 21:30

أَوَلَمْ يَرَ الَّذِينَ كَفَرُوا أَنَّ السَّمَوَاتِ وَالْأَرْضَ كَانَتَا رَتْقًا فَفَتَقْنَهُمَا وَجَعَلْنَا مِنَ الْمَاءِ كُلَّ شَيْءٍ حَيٍّ أَفَلَا يُؤْمِنُونَ

"Have not those who disbelieve known that the heavens and the earth were joined together as one united piece, then We parted them? And we have made every living thing from water. Will they not then believe?"

To better grasp this, we delve into the topic of the beginning of creation. The Quran in Surah Anbiya mentions that the heavens and the earth were initially joined together, then separated and that every living thing is created from water. This separation and creation from water marks significant aspects of Allah's creation process.

Hadith Source: Sunan al-Tirmidhī 3319

'Ubadah ibn As-Sāmit (may Allah be pleased with him) said to his son: "O Son, you will not taste true faith until you know that whatever has come to you would never have missed you, and that whatever has missed you would never have come to you. I heard the Messenger of Allah ﷺ say: 'The first thing Allah created was the Pen. He commanded it to write. It said: 'My Lord, what shall I write?' He said: 'Write down what has been ordained for all things until the establishment of the Hour."

O Son, I heard the Messenger of Allah ﷺ say: 'Whoever dies believing otherwise does not belong to me." In a narration by Imam

Ahmad: "Verily, the first thing Allah, the Almighty, created was the Pen. He said to it: 'Write.' So in that very hour it wrote down all what was to occur up to the Day of Judgment." In a narration by Ibn Wahb, the Messenger of Allah ﷺ said: "So, whoever disbelieved in fate, the good and the bad thereof, Allah will burn him with the Hellfire."

The pen wrote everything in a preserved tablet known as Al Louhul Mahfuds, which was written 50,000 years before Allah created the heavens and earth.

In Sahih Bukhari Volume 4, Book 54, Number 414, our beloved Prophet Muhammad ﷺ said that initially, there was only Allah, and then He created His Throne over the water, wrote everything in the Book, and subsequently created the heavens and the earth.

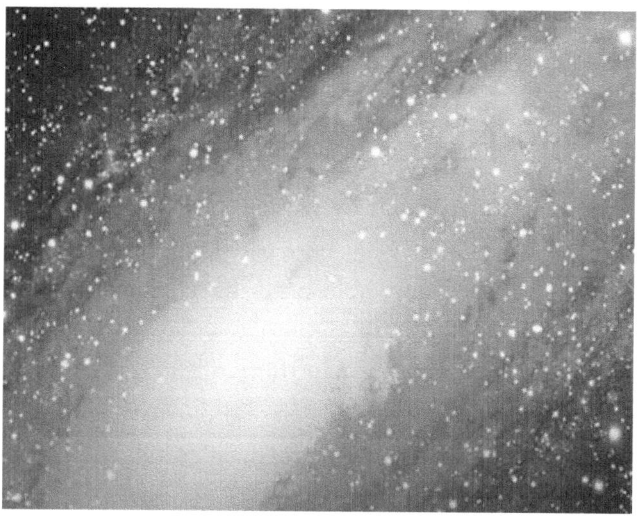

Suar Baqara 2: 22

الَّذِي جَعَلَ لَكُمُ الْأَرْضَ فِرَاشًا وَالسَّمَاءَ بِنَاءً وَأَنزَلَ مِنَ السَّمَاءِ مَاءً فَأَخْرَجَ بِهِ مِنَ الثَّمَرَاتِ رِزْقًا لَّكُمْ فَلَا تَجْعَلُوا لِلَّهِ أَندَادًا وَأَنتُمْ تَعْلَمُونَ

"Who has made the earth a resting place for you, and the sky as a canopy, and sent down water (precipitation) from the sky and brought forth therewith fruits as a provision for you. Then do not set up rivals unto Allâh (in worship) while you know (that He Alone has the right to be worshipped).

Concept Of Time in The Universe

The concept of time in the universe, as understood from Quranic verses like those in the chapters of Hajj and Maa'rij, highlights that time is not the same across the cosmos. Different regions experience time differently, a fact affirmed by scientific understanding.

The Quran mentions the creation of the earth and sky in six days. As stated in the Quran, "A day to your Lord equals a thousand years." Angels and the Ruh ascend towards Him in a day equivalent to fifty thousand years. There are instances where a day is equal to a thousand years and others where it's fifty thousand years.

Concerning the creation of the heavens, the Quran discusses multiple skies and the coexistence of darkness and light, highlighting the vastness and complexity of Allah's creation. Our understanding of stars and galaxies adds to the appreciation of the universe's immense scale.

Surah Al-Hajj 22:47

وَإِنَّ يَوْمًا عِندَ رَبِّكَ كَأَلْفِ سَنَةٍ مِّمَّا تَعُدُّونَ

And indeed, a day with your Lord is like a thousand years of those which you count.

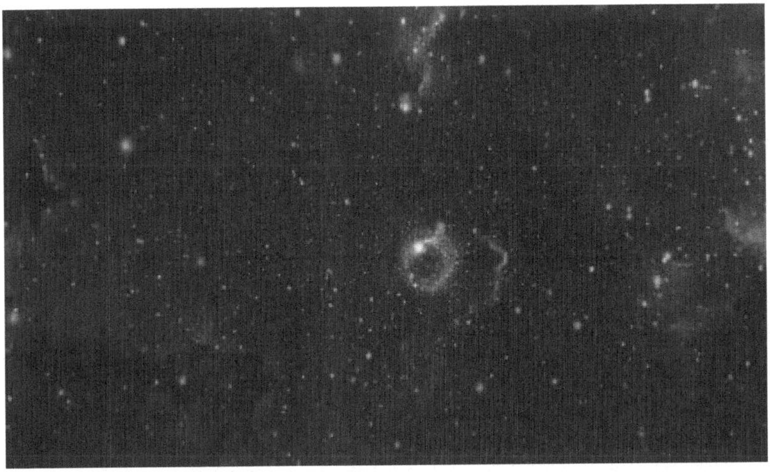

Surah Al-Maarij 70:4

تَعْرُجُ الْمَلَ كَةُ وَالرُّوحُ إِلَيْهِ فِي يَوْمٍ كَانَ مِقْدَارُهُ, خَمْسِينَ أَلْفَ سَنَةٍ

The angels and the Spirit will ascend to Him during a Day the extent of which is fifty thousand years

Creation Of Skies and Earth

The first verse of the chapter of Al-Anam is, "All praise is to Allah who created skies and the earth and the lights and the darknesses"

It indicates the existence of multiple skies and also the creation of darkness. The initial sky refers to the sky encompassing the Earth. The sun, being a star, is 1.3 million times the size of Earth, allowing for 1.3 million earths to fit within it. Beyond the sun, there are billions of stars, many larger than the sun. Creating a single galaxy requires millions of stars, and there are countless galaxies in existence. The expansive view we have of the sky reveals countless galaxies, each representing the first heaven. Allah is the Creator of seven heavens.

The Quran's portrayal of the seven heavens and their vast distances provides us with insight into the magnificence of Allah's creation. The comparison between the Kursi and 'Arsh further emphasizes the immense grandeur of Allah's ultimate Throne, showcasing the insignificance of the heavens in comparison.

The distance between one heaven to another heaven is 500 years. After the 7th heaven, we have the kursi of Allah/ footstool or chair of Allah.

Surah Al-Burooj 85:1

وَالسَّمَاءِ ذَاتِ الْبُرُوجِ

By the sky containing great stars

The analogy given by Prophet Muhammad ﷺ about the seven heavens and the size of Allah's Kursi and Arsh provides us with a way to grasp their magnitude. He likened the comparison of the seven heavens to a ring in a vast desert, emphasizing how minuscule they are in comparison to Allah's immense Throne. The concept is like throwing a tiny ring into the vast expanse of the Sahara Desert, highlighting the vastness of Allah's creations. Similarly, the Kursi is depicted as no more significant compared to the 'Arsh than a small ring thrown into a desert.

The Messenger of Allah ﷺ mentioned regarding the great throne of Allah Almighty, "...The Arsh is over the water, and Allah is over the 'Arsh, and He knows what you do." The 'Arsh is the greatest of all things that Allah has created, over which our Lord rose in a manner that befits His Majesty. This analogy underscores the immense scale of Allah's creation, from the lowest heaven to the highest, each level resembling a small ring in comparison to the vastness of the heavens and the Throne.

Sky According to Science and Islam

Let's return to our first sky which we see from earth and what science says about it. The troposphere, an atmospheric layer, is six and a half miles above us. Above that is the stratosphere, which is 31 miles thick and contains the ozone layer, protecting us from the sun's harmful rays. Beyond that, there's the mesosphere, which is 53 miles thick, and humans can't survive there because of extremely low temperatures reaching -90 degrees Celsius. Above that is the thermosphere, which is 300 miles thick. Beyond the thermosphere lies the Karman Line, an imaginary boundary marking the start of outer space. Beyond this line, the vast expanse of space begins.

Let's see what we find in Islam. Roman Emperor Heraclius wrote a letter to Mu'awiya(رضي الله عنه)carrying a question about "mujarra." Mu'awiya(رضي الله عنه)then forwarded that letter to Ibn Abbas (رضي الله عنه)so that he could provide a better answer. Ibn Abbas (رضي الله عنه) explained that "mujarra" is like a door in the sky, acting as a barrier between "here" and "there." It is a type of barrier through which nothing can pass, not even heat or temperature.

The Gates of Skies

Al-Mi'raj: Ascending Through the Gates of the Heavens

The Prophet ﷺ says Jibril عَلَيْهِ السَّلَامُ asked permission for the door of the heaven to open." The gatekeeper asked, "Who is it?" "It is Jibril." "Do you have anyone with you?" "Yes, I have with me, Muhammadﷺ." "Has he been sent for (does he have permission to pass)?" "Yes." And then the door opened up. And for every one of the seven heavens, this same conversation happened with each gatekeeper.

This shows that there are locked doors to the heavens, and each door has a gatekeeper. And the gatekeeper is not allowed to let anyone pass unless they have permission.

Creation of Angels and Jinn

So far, we've discussed the creation of heavens and earth. After forming skies and earth, Allah created angels, known as "Malaika." It is a fundamental aspect of our faith to believe in angels. Hadith Şahih Muslim 2996 Aisha (رضي الله عنه) reported: The Messenger of Allah, peace and blessings be upon him, said, "The angels were created from light, the Jinn were created from a mixture of fire, and Adam عَلَيْهِ السَّلَام was created as has been described for you." Angel Jibreel عَلَيْهِ السَّلَامُ was the first living creature to be created and brought into existence, even before Hellfire and Paradise were created. It is clear from a hadith

It was narrated from Abu Hurairah that the Messenger of Allah said: "When Allah created Paradise and Hell, He sent Jibril, peace be upon him, to Paradise and said: 'Look at it and at what I have prepared for its people in it.' He looked at it, then he came back and said: 'By Your Glory, no one will hear of it but he will enter it.' So He commanded that it be surrounded by hardships and said: 'Go and look at it and at what I have prepared for its people in it.' He looked at it and saw that it had been surrounded by hardships. He (Jibril) said: 'By Your Glory, I fear that no one will enter it.' He (Allah) said: 'Go and look at the Fire and at what I have prepared for its people in it.' So he looked at it and parts of it were piled upon other parts. He came back and said: 'By Your Glory, no one will enter it.' So He commanded that it be surrounded with pleasures and said: 'Go and look at it.' So he looked at it and saw that it was surrounded by pleasures. He came back and said: 'By Your Glory, I fear that no one will be saved from it and all will enter it. ""

Jibreel عَلَيْهِ السَّلَامُ is known by many names such as Roohul Quds (Holy Spirit), Roohul Amin (Trustworthy Spirit), etc. The first words he uttered after being brought to existence were "La hawla wa la quwwata illa billah". When Jibreel عَلَيْهِ السَّلَامُ took human form, he resembled Dihya bin Kalbi (رضي الله عنه) Dihya bin Kalbi was one of the most handsome men amongst the Companions of Muhammad ﷺ and was famously called the Yusuf of Banu Kalb (referring to how handsome Prophet Yusuf عَلَيْهِ السَّلَامُ was in his time).

The Prophet ﷺ says he saw Jibreel عَلَيْهِ السَّلَامُ in his original form only twice. Jibreel عَلَيْهِ السَّلَامُhad 600 wings, with pearls, rubies, and diamonds dripping from each wing. He filled up the entire horizon and was seen sitting on the throne that Allah provided for him. The colors of his wings and the soles of his feet were green. (Ahmad in al- Musnad, and Ibn Katheer said in al-Bidayah that its isnad (chain of narrators) is jayyid (good))

The nature and intensity of the revelation that was sent from Allah to Prophet Muhammad ﷺ through Jibreel عَلَيْهِ السَّلَامُwas such that angels would faint because of the sound they would hear. After regaining consciousness, they would ask Jibreel عَلَيْهِ السَّلَامُ what the sound was and Jibreel عَلَيْهِ السَّلَامُ would say "Haqq". (Abu Dawood(The Prophet ﷺ said the Revelation was like the ringing of a bell and then he would remember what Jibreel)عَلَيْهِ السَّلَامُ had brought to him from Allah (SWT). Sometimes He ﷺ would lose consciousness and sweat even on a cold day. Such was the intensity of the revelation, and Jibreel عَلَيْهِ السَّلَامُ was given the noblest task of delivering the wahi to the Prophet ﷺ

The Qur'an also speaks of angels as playing a crucial role in processes like creation, prophecy, spiritual life, death, resurrection, and the workings of natural elements. For instance, there is an angel who brings the thunder, and he, too, serves God and obeys His command. Other angels are in charge of embryos in wombs, or responsible for protecting human beings.

The Qur'an speaks of the charge of the angel of death in these verses:

Surah As-Sajda 32:11

قُلْ يَتَوَفَّىٰكُم مَّلَكُ الْمَوْتِ الَّذِي وُكِّلَ بِكُمْ ثُمَّ إِلَىٰ رَبِّكُمْ تُرْجَعُونَ

Say, "The angel of death will take you who has been entrusted with you. Then to your Lord, you will be returned."

The Qur'an also mentions angels in connection with Heaven and Hell:

Surah Al-Rad 13;23-24

جَنَّٰتُ عَدْنٍ يَدْخُلُونَهَا وَمَن صَلَحَ مِنْ ءَابَآئِهِمْ وَأَزْوَٰجِهِمْ وَذُرِّيَّٰتِهِمْ وَالْمَلَٰٓئِكَةُ يَدْخُلُونَ
عَلَيْهِم مِّن كُلِّ بَابٍ (٢٣) سَلَٰمٌ عَلَيْكُم بِمَا صَبَرْتُمْ فَنِعْمَ عُقْبَى الدَّارِ

Gardens of perpetual residence; they will enter them with whoever were righteous among their fathers, their spouses, and their descendants. And the angels will enter upon them from every gate, [saying], (23) "Peace be upon you for what you patiently endured. And excellent is the final home." (24)

Also, angels record the deeds of humans as long as they are on Earth:

Surah Al-Infitar 82: 10-12

وَإِنَّ عَلَيْكُمْ لَحَافِظِينَ (١٠) كِرَامًا كَاتِبِينَ (١١) يَعْلَمُونَ مَا تَفْعَلُونَ

And indeed, [appointed] over you are keepers, (10) Noble and recording; (11) They know whatever you do. (12)

Surah At-Tariq 86:4

إِن كُلُّ نَفْسٍ لَّمَّا عَلَيْهَا حَافِظٌ

There is no soul but it has over it a protector.

Angels are also mentioned in many hadiths. For example, the Prophet Muhammad ﷺ (peace be upon him) is reported to have said that when people gather together in remembrance of God, "The angels surround them, mercy covers them, peace descends on them, and God remembers them among those who are with Him" (At-Tirmidhi).

Human Eyesight and Hearing

Why can't we see Angels and Jinn? According to science, humans cannot see everything. If you read about the visible spectrum, you will understand this concept. The visible spectrum of light is the part of the electromagnetic spectrum that humans can see. I'm not here to teach you science, but understanding this spectrum will show you how limited human eyesight is. If humans could see beyond this spectrum, they would be exposed to harmful radiation and likely not survive. Out of 100%, humans can only see 0.0035%, which means that 99.9965% of the universe is hidden from us. This limitation is due to the extremely high frequencies of other radiation, which can harm our health. This is why in Surah Rehmaan, Allah says

فَبِأَيِّ آلَاءِ رَبِّكُمَا تُكَذِّبَانِ

"So which of the favors of your Lord would you deny?"

Similar constraints apply to human hearing. We have a limited range of hearing, and exceeding this range can cause harm, such as bleeding ears or even death. An example from the Quran illustrates this point: the people of Thamud were destroyed for disobeying Allah and his prophet Salih عَلَيْهِ السَّلَامُ They killed a she-camel that was miraculously created from rock, and as punishment, Allah destroyed them with a powerful sound wave that left them dead, as if they had never lived.

The Concept of Khalifa

After making angels and Jinn, Allah decided to create humans. Before creating Adam عَلَيْهِ السَّلَام Allah informed the angels that He would appoint a successor on Earth.

Sura Baqara 2:30

"And [mention, O Muhammad ﷺ], when your Lord said to the angels, 'Indeed, I will make upon the earth a khalifa (successive authority).' They said, 'Will You place upon it one who causes corruption therein and sheds blood, while we declare Your praise and sanctify You?' Allah said, 'Indeed, I know that which you do not know.'"

Khalifa can mean the passing on of responsibilities from one generation to the next, especially within families. For example, when a grandfather passes away, his son takes over as the new head of the family. This passing down of duties happens in families all the time, as parents give their children responsibilities that they will one day pass on to their kids.

The second meaning of the word Khalifa is an interesting one.

"Khalifa" can also mean someone left to their own devices and made in charge of another person. Now, the other person uses those devices because they are in charge and have the freedom to do whatever they want. If they were told not to lie but they are in charge, they can lie or not because they are in charge for the time being. Allah has given us some time, and we are responsible for making decisions. Whoever is doing good will get paradise, and whoever is doing bad will get hell. For the time being, we are Khalifa.

Allah says to the angels that He will put someone on this Earth whom He will leave to make their own decisions. Allah is not going to force any decision on you; you're going to have to decide whether you want to wake up and pray or not; you're going to decide that.

The third meaning is that we will not take any of this stuff with us we don't even own our physical bodies. This body will be testifying against us on Judgment Day we don't own it. We have been in charge of this body for some time. But this body is technically not ours and Allah will take it back too.

(Surah Al-Baqarah, Quran 2:31)

وَعَلَّمَ ءَادَمَ الْأَسْمَاءَ كُلَّهَا ثُمَّ عَرَضَهُمْ عَلَى الْمَلَٰئِكَةِ فَقَالَ أَنْبِئُونِي بِأَسْمَاءِ هَٰؤُلَاءِ إِن كُنتُمْ صَٰدِقِينَ

And He taught Adam عَلَيْهِ السَّلَام the names all of them. Then He showed them to the angels and said, "Inform Me of the names of these, if you are truthful."

Allah taught Adam عَلَيْهِ السَّلَام the names of all things. Then He presented those things to the angels and the angels could not know the names of those things. So the first difference between Adam عَلَيْهِ السَّلَام and the angels is that Adam عَلَيْهِ السَّلَام can obtain knowledge. That's very important for the rest of the story. Adam عَلَيْهِ السَّلَام can learn whereas the angels could not learn of their own free will. They did not have free will like Adam عَلَيْهِ السَّلَام had. So the differentiating factor was this knowledge which the angels could only obtain through direct inspiration from Allah. That is why Jibril was just a messenger. There is no way that Jibril could add anything to the Quran or subtract anything from the Quran because his knowledge was directly inspired by Allah and he takes it to the Prophet ﷺ. That is his role, that is his duty,...

Earth Dwellers Before Adam عَلَيْهِ السَّلَام

The angels could not understand Allah's objective for this creation. Based only on what they were told, angels thought that if a creation with free will were given some authority on earth, it would cause chaos on earth, disrupt the natural balance of the ecology, shed blood, waste life, and spread corruption. They had already observed misuse of freedom on the part of Jinns. So, they respectfully shared their concern to learn about Allah SWT's wisdom.

In Quran Allah says: Surely I know what you do not know. And He taught Adam عَلَيْهِ السَّلَام all the names, then presented them to the angels and said: Tell me about their names if you are right. They said: Glory be to You; we do not know whatever You have taught us; surely You are the Knowing, the Wise He said: Adam عَلَيْهِ السَّلَام tell them their names. Then when he had informed them of their names, Allah said: "Did I not say to you that I know everything about the heavens and the earth which are beyond your range of knowledge and I know all that you disclose and also all that you hide?

Before I dive into telling you how Allah taught Adam عَلَيْهِ السَّلَامall the names, I want to talk about how Allah made Adam عَلَيْهِ السَّلَامin the first place.

It is mentioned in the Quran that our father, Adam عَلَيْهِ السَّلَام was created with the earth's clay. The Quran says Allah created everything with water.

Surah Al-Furqan 25: 54

وَهُوَ الَّذِي خَلَقَ مِنَ الْمَاءِ بَشَرًا فَجَعَلَهُ, نَسَبًا وَصِهْرًا وَكَانَ رَبُّكَ قَدِيرًا ٥٤

And it is He Who has created man from water,

Quran also says we are created from Turaab- dry dust

Surah Kahf 18: 37

قَالَ لَهُ صَاحِبُهُ، وَهُوَ يُحَاوِرُهُ أَكَفَرْتَ بِالَّذِي خَلَقَكَ مِن تُرَابٍ ثُمَّ مِن نُّطْفَةٍ ثُمَّ سَوَّىٰكَ رَجُلًا ٣٧

"Do you disbelieve in the One Who created you from dust,

Surah Al-Room 30: 20

وَمِنْ ءَايَٰتِهِۦٓ أَنْ خَلَقَكُم مِّن تُرَابٍ ثُمَّ إِذَآ أَنتُم بَشَرٌ تَنتَشِرُونَ ٢٠

One of His signs is that He created you from dust, then-behold!- you are human beings spreading over the earth'.

The Quran also says that man was created from earth

Surah Nooh 71: 17

وَاللَّهُ أَنۢبَتَكُم مِّنَ الْأَرْضِ نَبَاتًا ١٧

And Allah has caused you to grow from the earth a [progressive] growth.

Surah Al-Anaam 6:2

هُوَ الَّذِي خَلَقَكُم مِّن طِينٍ ثُمَّ قَضَىٰٓ أَجَلًا وَأَجَلٌ مُّسَمًّى عِندَهُۥ ۖ ثُمَّ أَنتُمْ تَمْتَرُونَ

It is He who created you from clay (teen)

The Quran also says that Allah created us from Salsaal

Surah Ar-Rahman 55: 14

خَلَقَ الْإِنسَانَ مِن صَلْصَالٍ كَالْفَخَّارِ ١٤

He created man from clay like [that of] pottery. (14)

Salsaal means clay that has been dried. Teen means wet clay

In short, Man was created from Turab, Ard, Teen, and Salsaal, these four are different forms of water and sand

- Turab- Sand with no water
- Ard- Sand with a little bit of water
- Teen- Sand with a lot of water
- Salsaal- Mix sand and water and leave it for a long time. When it dries, it turns into Salsaal.

Quran mentions in Surah Sa'ad, that Allah created the body of Adam عَلَيْهِ السَّلَام with his own hands.

Surah Sad 38:75

قَالَ يَٰإِبْلِيسُ مَا مَنَعَكَ أَن تَسْجُدَ لِمَا خَلَقْتُ بِيَدَىَّ أَسْتَكْبَرْتَ أَمْ كُنتَ مِنَ الْعَالِينَ

[Allah] said, "O Iblees, what prevented you from prostrating to that which I created with My hands?

Hadith. [Kitab at-Tawheed, Sahih al-Bukhari No. 7440]

The Prophet (peace and blessings be upon him) has informed us by way of Anas: The Prophet (peace and blessings be upon him) said, "The believers will be kept (waiting) on the Day of Resurrection so long that they will become worried and say, "Let us ask somebody to intercede for us with our Lord so that He may relieve us from our place.

Then they will go to Adam عَلَيْهِ السَّلَام and say, "You are Adam عَلَيْهِ السلام the father of the people. Allah created you with His Own Hand and made you reside in His Paradise and ordered His angels to prostrate before you, and taught you the names of all things will you intercede for us with your Lord so that He may relieve us from this place of ours? Adam عَلَيْهِ السَّلَام will say, 'I am not fit for this undertaking.' He will mention the error which he committed, i.e., his eating off the tree though he had been forbidden to do so. He will add Go to Noah عَلَيْهِ السَّلَام the first prophet sent by Allah to the people of the Earth.'

The people will go to Noah عَلَيْهِ السَّلَام who will say, I am not fit for this undertaking' He will mention the error which he committed, i.e., his asking his Lord without knowledge.' He will say (to them), 'Go to Abraham, Khalil ar-Rahman عَلَيْهِ السَّلَام They will go to Abraham عَلَيْهِ السَّلَام who will say, 'I am not fit for this undertaking. He would mention three words by which he was evasive, and say (to them). 'Go to Musa عَلَيْهِ السَّلَام slave whom Allah gave the Torah and spoke to directly and brought near Him, for conversation.'

They will go to Musa عَلَيْهِ السَّلَام who will say, 'I am not fit for this undertaking. He will mention his error which he committed, i.e., killing a person, and will say (to them) go to Isa عَلَيْهِ السَّلَام Allah's slave and His messenger, and a soul created by Him and His Word "Be: And it is". They will go to Isa عَلَيْهِ السَّلَام who will say, 'I am not fit for this undertaking but you'd better go to Muhammad ﷺ whose past and future sins have been forgiven by Allah.' So they will come to me, and I will ask my Lord's permission to enter His presence and then I will be permitted.

When I see Him I will fall down in prostration before Him, and He will leave me (in prostration) as long as He wills, and then He will say, 'O Muhammad, lift up your head and speak, for you will be listened to, and intercede, for your intercession will be accepted, and ask (for anything) for it will be granted:'

Then I will raise my head and glorify my Lord with certain praises which He has taught me. Allah will put a limit for me (to intercede for a certain type of people) I will take them out and make them enter Paradise." (Qatada said: I heard Anas saying that), the Prophet (peace and blessings be upon him) said, "I will go out and take them out of Hell (Fire) and let them enter Paradise, and then I will return and ask my Lord for permission to enter His presence and I will be permitted.

When I see Him I will fall down in prostration before Him and He will leave me in prostration as long as He wants me (in that state), and then He will say, 'O Muhammad, raise your head and speak, for you will be listened to, and intercede, for your intercession will be accepted, and ask, your request will be granted.' " The Prophet (Prayers and blessing of Allah be upon him) added, "So I will raise my head and glorify and praise Him as He has taught me.

Then I will intercede and He will put a limit for me (to intercede for a certain type of people). I will take them out and let them enter Paradise." (Qatada added: I heard Anas saying that) The Prophet

said, 'I will go out and take them out of Hell (Fire) and let them enter Paradise, and I will return for the third time and will ask my Lord for permission to enter His presence and I will be allowed to enter.

When I see Him, I will fall down in prostration before Him and will remain in prostration as long as He will, and then He will say, 'Raise your head, O Muhammad, and speak, for you will be listened to, and intercede, for your intercession will be accepted, and ask, for your request will be granted.' So I will raise my head and praise Allah as He has taught me and then I will intercede and He will put a limit for me (to intercede for a certain type of people). I will take them out and let them enter Paradise."

(Qatada said: I heard Anas saying that) the Prophet (Prayers and blessing of Allah be upon him) said, "So I will go out and take them out of Hell (Fire) and let them enter Paradise, till none will remain in the Fire except those whom Qur'an will imprison (i.e., those who are destined for eternal life in the fire)." The narrator then recited the Verse:- "It may be that your Lord will raise you to a Station of Praise and Glory.' (17.79) The narrator added: This is the Station of Praise and Glory which Allah has promised to your Prophet.

From this Hadith, it is clear that Allah created Adam عَلَيْهِ السَّلَام with HIS Hands.

According to a hadith in Tirmdhi, the creation of Adam عَلَيْهِ السَّلَام started with a handful of dirt from the entire earth and this is the reason why his offspring has different colors and different natures and then with the extract of that dirt, whose true nature is known only to Allah the Adam عَلَيْهِ السَّلَام was created and according to surah Sa'ad, Allah created the body of Adam عَلَيْهِ السَّلَام with his own hands and according to hadith, as long as he will he let the body be there where it was created and it was then when Iblees used to visit his body to figure out its true nature according to ibn Abbas Adam عَلَيْهِ السَّلَام's body was left there for forty days according to a hadith in Muslim, Allah ordered that body to be alive on Friday between the time of evening and night, the body was given soul and it became alive.

Adam عَلَيْهِ السَّلَام sneezed when the soul was given and the first words Adam عَلَيْهِ السَّلَام uttered were "praise to Allah" and Allah replied with "May Allah have mercy on you" As the soul started to penetrate the body, the body turned into flesh and blood from clay and when it reached to the belly button Adam عَلَيْهِ السَّلَام felt happy and wanted to stand up but he could not and it was this haste mentioned in Quran

Surah Isra'a Ayah 11

وَكَانَ الْإِنْسَانُ عَجُولًا

"Indeed, the human makes haste."

The soul had not yet reached his feet that he wanted to walk.

What is the Ruh

What the Quran says about the Ruh.

In Quran Sura Isra 17:85

وَيَسْئَلُونَكَ عَنِ الرُّوحِ قُلِ الرُّوحُ مِنْ أَمْرِ رَبِّى وَمَا أُوتِيْتُمْ مِّنَ الْعِلْمِ إِلَّا قَلِيلًا

And they ask you [O Muhammad ﷺ] concerning the Ruh [the spirit]. Say: 'The Ruh: it is one of the things, the knowledge of which is only with my Lord. And of knowledge, you (mankind) have been given only a little.

This Aayah of the Quran was revealed when some Jews asked our prophet ﷺ question about Ruh. The following hadith is about the incident when the Jews asked Prophet Muhammad ﷺ about Ruh

(Soul) and the Prophet replied after getting the divine inspiration.

Sahi Bukhari 104.

Narrated Abdullah bin Mas'ûd -: While I was going with the Prophetﷺ through the ruins of Al-Madîna and he was reclining on a date- palm leaf stalk, some Jews passed by. Some of them said to the others; Ask him (the Prophetﷺ) about the Rûh (the spirit). Some of them said that they should not ask him that question as he might give a reply which would displease them. But some of them insisted on asking, and so one of them stood up and asked, O Abâl-Qasim! What is the Rûh (the spirit)?" The Prophet ﷺ remained quiet. I thought he was being inspired divinely.

So I stayed till that state of the Prophet (while being inspired) was over. The Prophet ﷺ then said, Quran "And they ask you (O Muhammad ﷺ concerning the Rûh (the spirit) Say; The Rûh (the spirit) its knowledge is with my Lord. And of knowledge, you (mankind) have been given, only a little". [Quran, Surah al-Israa 17:85]"

Regarding ruh, its knowledge is with Allah so we will not talk much about it. Only I will write one thing Some of the scholars held this view that Allah first created Noor/light. When Allah says to it: "Be!" - and it is.

Sura baqara Aayah 117

بَدِيعُ السَّمَوَاتِ وَالْأَرْضِ وَإِذَا قَضَى أَمْرًا فَإِنَّمَا يَقُولُ لَهُ كُن فَيَكُونُ و

The Originator of the heavens and the earth. When He decrees a matter, He only says to it: "Be!" - and it is.

With that powerful word كُن Noor was created and with Noor soul and angels were created. But we do not know its authenticity. And Allah knows best.

In Hadith Tirmidhi 3076

Narrated Abu Hurairah: the Messenger of Allah (ﷺ) said: "When Allah created Adam عَلَيْهِ السَّلَام He wiped his back and every person that He created among his offspring until the Day of Resurrection fell out of his back. He placed a ray of light between the eyes of every person. Then He showed them to Adam عَلَيْهِ السَّلَام and he said: 'O Lord! Who are these people?' He said: 'These are your offspring.' He saw one of them whose ray between his eyes amazed him, so he said: 'O Lord! Who is this?' He said: 'This is a man from the latter nations of your offspring called Dawud.' He said: 'Lord! How long did You make his lifespan?' He said: 'Sixty years.' He said: 'O Lord! Add forty years from my life to his.' So at the end of Adam عَلَيْهِ السَّلَامlife, the Angel of Death came to him, and he said: 'Do I not have forty years remaining?' He said: 'Did you not give them to your son Dawud?" He said: "Adam عَلَيْهِ السَّلَام denied so his offspring denied, and Adam عَلَيْهِ السَّلَام forgot and his offspring forgot, and Adam عَلَيْهِ السَّلَام sinned, so his offspring sinned."

Surah Al-Araf Aayah 172

وَإِذْ أَخَذَ رَبُّكَ مِنْ بَنِي عَادَمَ مِن ظُهُورِهِمْ ذُرِّيَّتَهُمْ وَأَشْهَدَهُمْ عَلَى أَنفُسِهِمْ أَلَسْتُ بِرَبِّكُمْ قَالُوا بَلَى شَهِدْنَا أَن تَقُولُوا يَوْمَ الْقِيَمَةِ إِنَّا كُنَّا عَنْ هَذَا غَفِلِينَ

And (remember) when your Lord brought forth from the Children of Adam عَلَيْهِ السَّلَام from their loins, their seed (or from Adam عَلَيْهِ السلام s loin his offspring) and made them testify as to themselves (saying): "Am I not your Lord?" They said: "Yes! We testify," lest you should say on the Day of Resurrection: "Verily, we have been unaware of this."

According to the Hadith and the Quran, it is mentioned that Allah SWT touched the backbone of Adam عَلَيْهِ السَّلَام and from the backbone, he extracted every single soul that will be in existence till the day of judgment. Our souls were created and we declared that Allah is our creator when Allah asked us Alasti bi rabbikum don't you know I am your Rubb we replied Balaa, "Yes indeed you are our Rubb".

A beautiful hadith about the soul with a slight variation of words, a companion of a prophet named Abu Hurayra رضي الله عنه reports that in the realm of souls, our souls lived in groups the souls that were familiar to each other in that realm also recognize each other in this realm and the souls unfamiliar to each other in that realm stay unfamiliar to each other in this one.

One important point to note is that Allah breathed the soul into Adam عَلَيْهِ السَّلَام and for the rest of us, our souls were extracted from the backbone of Adam عَلَيْهِ السَّلَام

Stages of Ruh

There are five stages of Ruh

1. The first stage is up there which is clear in surah Aa'raf where all souls bear witness that Allah is our Master. Ruh of all who will come to this world till the day of judgment is already created up there and we have no information about it where are they right now.

2. The second stage is in the mother's womb.

This is clear by the following hadith

"The Messenger of Allah (peace and blessings of Allah be upon him), who is the most truthful (of human beings) and his being truthful (is a fact) told us: The constituents of one of you are gathered in his mother's womb for forty days, then it becomes a clot of blood within another period of forty days. Then it becomes a lump of flesh, and forty days later, Allah sends His angel to it to breathe into it the soul. The angel comes with instructions concerning four things, so the

angel writes down his livelihood, his death, his deeds, and whether he will doomed or blessed." (Reported by Muslim, 1528).

We know that Allah breathes into the body of Adam عَلَيْهِ السَّلَامُ Ruh. This was special for Adam عَلَيْهِ السَّلَامُ For everyone else when we were in our mothers' wombs as a lump of flash Allah sends His angel to it to breathe into the soul.

The third stage is in this world, what we are passing through right now the stage of our soul, spent in this world.

Now the question arises: Why have we forgotten the oath we made with Allah?

If we remember everything then a test of this world would have become meaningless. Allah says in

Sura Mulk ayah 2

الَّذِي خَلَقَ الْمَوْتَ وَالْحَيَوٰةَ لِيَبْلُوَكُمْ أَيُّكُمْ أَحْسَنُ عَمَلاً وَهُوَ الْعَزِيزُ الْغَفُورُ

we created life and death to test you.

And Allah also says in **Sura baqara Aayah 3**

الَّذِينَ يُؤْمِنُونَ بِالْغَيْبِ وَيُقِيمُونَ الصَّلَاةَ وَمِمَّا رَزَقْنَاهُمْ يُنفِقُونَ

Who believe in the Ghaib/unseen. They are on (true) guidance from their Lord, and they are successful.

We all forgot that we once declared Allah as our Master. This memory is hidden in our subconscious mind but removed from our conscious memory to test us in this life.

The fourth stage is when death comes to our bodies.

During sleep, the soul (ruh) temporarily departs from the body but returns upon waking. However, when the soul permanently leaves the body, the state of Barzakh begins.

Sura [Az-Zumar 39:42]

اللَّهُ يَتَوَفَّى الْأَنفُسَ حِينَ مَوْتِهَا وَالَّتِي لَمْ تَمُتْ فِي مَنَامِهَا فَيُمْسِكُ الَّتِي قَضَىٰ عَلَيْهَا الْمَوْتَ وَيُرْسِلُ الْأُخْرَىٰ إِلَىٰ أَجَلٍ مُّسَمًّى إِنَّ فِي ذَٰلِكَ لَآيَاتٍ لِّقَوْمٍ يَتَفَكَّرُونَ

"It is Allah Who takes away the souls at the time of their death and those that die not during their sleep. He keeps those (souls) for which He has ordained death and sends the rest for a term appointed. Verily, in this are signs for a people who think deeply."

Sura [Al-An'am 6:60]

وَهُوَ الَّذِي يَتَوَفَّاكُم بِاللَّيْلِ وَيَعْلَمُ مَا جَرَحْتُم بِالنَّهَارِ ثُمَّ يَبْعَثُكُمْ فِيهِ لِيُقْضَىٰ أَجَلٌ مُّسَمًّى ثُمَّ إِلَيْهِ مَرْجِعُكُمْ ثُمَّ يُنَبِّئُكُم بِمَا كُنتُمْ تَعْمَلُونَ

"It is He Who takes your souls by night (when you are asleep), and has knowledge of all that you have done by day."

In Hadith, Our Prophet ﷺ said sleeping is the brother of death.

Different souls have different places. Bad souls go to a place called Sijjeen.

Surah al-Mutafifeen, 83: 7

كَلَّا إِنَّ كِتَابَ الْفُجَّارِ لَفِي سِجِّينٍ

No! Indeed, the record of the wicked is in Sijjeen.

A good soul will have a different station. That station is illiyin. Ibn Qayyim al-Jawziyya has said that within illiyin there are three stages. According to a sahih hadith in Sahih Muslim, the one who dies a shaheed, Allah (swt) will put his/her soul into a green bird that roams freely in Paradise and they return to shelter to lamps beneath the Throne.

Our Prophet ﷺ also informed that the soul of a believer is a bird from paradise that eats from it until the day of resurrection comes and Allah returns it to its body.

4th stage is Barzakh that will last until the last trumpet.

5th stage starts when on the day of judgment all souls will return to their bodies.

Then the final stage of our soul, an eternal life. ruh with body (body of different world not body of this world) in the next world.

Fitrah

So far, we've talked about different stages of Ruuh. Now, let's go into more detail about the third stage: when Ruuh connects with the body, especially during the amazing process of childbirth.

The concept of the Fitrah comes from the Qur'an which states:

Surah Al-Room 30:30

فَأَقِمْ وَجْهَكَ لِلدِّينِ حَنِيفًا فِطْرَتَ اللَّهِ الَّتِي فَطَرَ النَّاسَ عَلَيْهَا لَا تَبْدِيلَ لِخَلْقِ اللَّهِ ذَٰلِكَ الدِّينُ الْقَيِّمُ وَلَٰكِنَّ أَكْثَرَ النَّاسِ لَا يَعْلَمُونَ

So direct your face toward the religion, inclining to truth. [Adhere to] the fitrah of Allah upon which He has created [all] people. No change should there be in the creation of Allah. That is the correct religion, but most of the people do not know. (30)

[Sahih Bukhari 1292 and Sahih Muslim 2658]

Abu Huraira reported: The Prophet (ﷺ) said: "Every child is born with the Fitrah. His parents then make him a Jew, a Christian, or a fire worshiper. If an animal gives birth to a youngster with intact limbs, do you see any error?"

Then Abu Huraira recited the Quran verse: "The Fitrah with which Allah created mankind".

[Sahih Muslim 2659a]

Abu Huraira reported: The Prophet (ﷺ) said: "The mother of each person gives birth to him according to his Fitrah. It is then his parents who make him a Jew, Christian, or fire worshiper. If his parents had been Muslim, he would have remained Muslim too.

From the Quran and hadith, it is clear that every child is born with Fitrah. Allah has created the Fitrah for us so that we can recognize and worship Allah. But the child is then changed by parents to a Christian, Jew, or other religion. Even as a child grows up in a Muslim family, Satan tries to lead them astray.

Anas ibn Malik reported: The Messenger of Allah ﷺ, peace and blessings be upon him, was in the company of one of his wives when a man passed by them. The Prophet ﷺ called to him and when he came, the Prophet said ﷺ, "She is my wife." The man said, "O Messenger of Allah ﷺ, I do not doubt you in the least." The Prophet ﷺ said, "Verily, Satan flows through the human being like blood."

Source: Sahih Muslim 2174

From the above hadith, it is clear that life is about choices. In the third stage, we exist as a combination of soul (Rooh) and body. The nature of the soul, or Fitra, inclines us towards good, while the nature of the body, or Nafs, inclines us towards bad. Life is a struggle between Nafs and Fitra. Satan tempts the Nafs to do wrong, but the Fitra urges us to do right. Thus, life revolves around making choices between good and bad decisions.

Our Nafs adopt a wrong path and develop impurities then we cleanse our Nafs and it becomes pure again. Then again it becomes impure and we cleanse it again. The problem is with Nafs and not with human nature because we know every child is born with Fitrah.

Different Types of Nafs

The Quran speaks of different types of Nafs. It sometimes refers to Nafs-e-Ammara, Nafs-e-Lawwama, and Nafs-e-Mutmainna.

Quran calls Nafs e Ammara in **Sura Yusuf 12:53**

وَمَا أُبَرِّئُ نَفْسِي إِنَّ النَّفْسَ لَأَمَّارَةٌ

"And I free not myself (from the blame). Verily, the (human) self is inclined to evil, except when my Lord bestows His Mercy (upon whom He wills). Verily, my Lord is Oft-Forgiving, Most Merciful." (53)

Nafs e Ammara seeks the pleasures of this world and embraces such characteristics as self-admiration and self-praise, arrogance and pride, lying, gossip and backbiting, envy and jealousy, criticism, dissatisfaction, selfishness, greed, and love of self. Muslims are urged to control such desires by treating others with humility, respect, dignity, and similar qualities.

Quran calls Nafs e Lawaamah in Sura Qiyamah

Surah Al-Qiyama 75: 1-2

لَا أُقْسِمُ بِيَوْمِ الْقِيَامَةِ (1) أُقْسِمُ بِالنَّفْسِ اللَّوَّامَةِ

I swear by the Day of Resurrection, (1) And I swear by the self-reproaching conscience

The Nafs Al-lawwama knows the excellence of good actions and keeps the self away from wrong actions and bad deeds: "I swear by the self-reproaching soul". Engaging in wrong actions produces guilt, which increases so much that the person begins to correct or avoid such actions so that he/she will stop feeling shame, embarrassment, and regret.

Quran calls Nafs e Mutmainna in **Sura Fajr 89: 27**

أَيَّتُهَا النَّفْسُ الْمُطْمَئِنَّةُ

It will be said to the pious believers of Islamic Monotheism): *"O (you) the one in (complete) rest and satisfaction!*

The Nafs al-Mutma'inna is a state of serenity, tranquility, and peace, for one has reached the stage where he/she no longer commits wrong actions and bad deeds: "As for you, O content soul, return to your Lord, pleased and pleasing".

Suhayb reported: The Messenger of Allah, peace and blessings be upon him, said, "Wondrous is the affair of a believer, as it is good for him in every matter; this is not the case for anyone but a believer. If he experiences pleasure, he thanks Allah and it is good for him. If he experiences harm, he shows patience and it is good for him." Source: Şahih Muslim 2999

Surah Ash-Shams 91:7-8

"By the One who brought the self to equilibrium inspiring it with its transgression and its consciousness" (7)

Anas ibn Malik reported: "The Prophet, peace and blessings be upon him, said, 'All of the children of Adam عَلَيْهِ السَّلام and Eve are sinners, and the best sinners are those who repent" ("Sunan al- Tirmidhi," hadith no. 2499).

Gift of Knowledge

So far we have discussed Rooh, Fitra, Nasf, and its types. Let us go back to our topic about Adam عَلَيْهِ السَّلَام After Adam عَلَيْهِ السلام was given a soul, he was also given a gift of knowledge. According to Quran Sura Baqara Aayah 31

وَعَلَّمَ ءَادَمَ الْأَسْمَاءَ كُلَّهَا ثُمَّ عَرَضَهُمْ عَلَى الْمَلَائِكَةِ فَقَالَ أَنْبِئُونِي بِأَسْمَاءِ هَؤُلَاءِ إِن كُنتُمْ صَادِقِينَ

And He taught Adam عَلَيْهِ السَّلَام all the names (of everything), then He showed them to the angels and said, "Tell Me the names of these if you are truthful." (31)

Allah taught Adam عَلَيْهِ السَّلَام the names of everything, their proper names, the names of their characteristics, and what they do. Adam عَلَيْهِ السَّلَام was shown all of us by name. We all were there besides Adam عَلَيْهِ السَّلَام We were souls but Adam عَلَيْهِ السَّلَام was with body and soul. Allah asked angels if they could give me the names of these things, and they replied that they didn't know anything except what you taught us. He called Adam عَلَيْهِ السَّلَام and he gave all names.

Sura Baqara Aayah 32

الُوا سُبْحَنَكَ لَا عِلْمَ لَنَا إِلَّا مَا عَلَّمْتَنَا إِنَّكَ أَنتَ الْعَلِيمُ الْحَكِيمُ

They (angels) said: "Glory be to You, we have no knowledge except what you have taught us. Verily, it is You, the All-Knower, the All- Wise."

Sura Baqara Aayah 33

قَالَ يَادَمُ أَنْبِئْهُم بِأَسْمَاءِ هِمْ فَلَمَّا أَنْبَأَهُم بِأَسْمَابِهِمْ قَالَ أَلَمْ أَقُل لَّكُمْ إِنِّي أَعْلَمُ غَيْبَ
السَّمَوَاتِ وَالْأَرْضِ وَأَعْلَمُ مَا تُبْدُونَ وَمَا كُنتُمْ تَكْتُمُونَ

He said: "O Adam عَلَيْهِ السَّلَام *Inform them of their names," and when he had informed them of their names, He said: "Did I not tell you that I know the Ghaib (unseen) in the heavens and the earth, and I know what you reveal and what you have been concealing?"*

Allah's statement means, "Tell Me the names of what I paraded before you, O angels who said, (Will You place therein those who will make mischief therein and shed blood). You asked, 'Are You appointing a Khalifah from us or from other creations We praise and glorify You.

Therefore, Allah said, "If you say the truth, that if I appoint a non- angel Khalifah on the earth, he and his offspring will disobey Me, commit mischief, and shed blood, but if I designate you the Khalifahs you will obey Me, follow My command and honor and glorify Me. However, since you do not know the names of the objects I paraded before you, then you have even less knowledge of what will occur on the earth that does not exist yet.

Angels' question expresses their wonderment, seeking a reason rather than doubting their Lord. Hence why Allah سُبْحَٰنَهُ وَتَعَٰلَىٰ responds, "Indeed, I know that which you do not know," and the verse continues to name how mankind would be bestowed with knowledge, to which the Angels then reply,

"Glory be to You! We have no knowledge except what You have taught us. You are truly the All-Knowing, All-Wise."

Surah Al-Baqara 2:34

وَإِذْ قُلْنَا لِلْمَلَٰٓئِكَةِ اسْجُدُوا لِآدَمَ فَسَجَدُوٓا إِلَّآ إِبْلِيسَ أَبَىٰ وَاسْتَكْبَرَ وَكَانَ مِنَ الْكَٰفِرِينَ

And (remember) when We said to the angels: "Prostrate yourselves before Adam عَلَيْهِ السَّلَام ". And they prostrated except Iblis (Satan), he refused and was proud and was one of the disbelievers (disobedient to Allâh)

Surah Al-Araf 7:11

وَلَقَدْ خَلَقْنَٰكُمْ ثُمَّ صَوَّرْنَٰكُمْ ثُمَّ قُلْنَا لِلْمَلَٰٓئِكَةِ اسْجُدُوا لِآدَمَ فَسَجَدُوٓا إِلَّآ إِبْلِيسَ لَمْ يَكُن مِّنَ السَّٰجِدِينَ

And surely, We created you (your father Adam عَلَيْهِ السَّلَام and then gave you shape (the noble shape of a human being); then We told the angels, "Prostrate yourselves to Adam عَلَيْهِ السَّلَام and they prostrated themselves, except Iblis (Satan), he refused to be of those who prostrated themselves.

Now, in this ayah, it gives the impression that Iblis was an angel. However, this confusion is cleared in Surah Kahf, verse 50, where Allah سُبْحَٰنَهُ وَتَعَٰلَىٰ says "And mention when We said to the angels, "Prostrate to Adam عَلَيْهِ السَّلَام and they prostrated, except for Iblees. He was of the Jinn and departed from the command of his Lord." This is how Iblees was able to refuse Allah's command, he has freedom of will just as we humans do.

Angels do not possess free will; they can question but do not have the freedom to choose. Free will is given to humans and Jinn, which is why all angels obey, while Iblis does not.

The question now is how Iblis was among the angels. Jinns have free will, allowing for both good and bad among them. When Iblis consistently made good choices, his status elevated until he reached the rank of the angels. Since Iblis was obedient to Allah just like the angels, he was permitted to hold a rank among them. When Allah asked the angels to bow to Adam عَلَيْهِ السَّلام Iblees was with them and refused to bow down even though he was given that command. He was arrogant and refused to prostrate.

Surah Al-Araf Aayah 7:12

قَالَ مَا مَنَعَكَ أَلَّا تَسْجُدَ إِذْ أَمَرْتُكَ قَالَ أَنَا خَيْرٌ مِّنْهُ خَلَقْتَنِي مِن نَّارٍ وَخَلَقْتَهُ مِن طين

(Allâh) said: "What prevented you (O Iblîs) that you did not prostrate yourself when I commanded you?" Iblîs said: "I am better than him (Adam عَلَيْهِ السَّلَام) You created me from fire, and him You created from clay."

Iblis concentrated solely on the physical aspect of humans, the clay while disregarding the spiritual dimension, the Ruh (soul). The lesson we can draw from this is that he aims to distract us by focusing only on our worldly life and neglecting the spiritual side. Additionally, Iblis encourages us to compare ourselves with others, as he did with Adam عَلَيْهِ السَّلَام This leads us to think like him, constantly questioning why others might have more whether it's a better job, more wealth, a beautiful home, or greater happiness prompting us to compare ourselves with others in various aspects of life.

Surah Al-Araf 7:13

قَالَ فَاهْبِطْ مِنْهَا فَمَا يَكُونُ لَكَ أَن تَتَكَبَّرَ فِيهَا فَاخْرُجْ إِنَّكَ مِنَ الصَّغِرِينَ

(Allâh) said: "(O Iblîs) get down from this (Paradise), it is not for you to be arrogant here. Get out, for you are of those humiliated and disgraced."

Satan is insignificant and worthless, but we often think he is controlling us. In reality, he can only lead us astray. If we hold fast to the Book of Allah and recite "A'udhu billahi min ash-shaytan ir-rajim" (I seek refuge with Allah from the accursed Satan), he loses his power over us.

Surah Al-Araf 7:14

قَالَ أَنظِرْنِي إِلَىٰ يَوْمِ يُبْعَثُونَ

(Iblîs) said: "Allow me respite till the Day they are raised up (i.e. the Day of Resurrection).

Allah created the earth and intended to appoint a khalifa (representative) on it who would make their own choices. If we make good choices, we will pass this test on the Day of Judgment and be granted entry into heaven. We all agreed to come to earth, undergo this test, and then seek our place in heaven.

This is clear from Sura Ahzab

Surah Al-Ahzab 33:72

إِنَّا عَرَضْنَا الْأَمَانَةَ عَلَى السَّمَوَاتِ وَالْأَرْضِ وَالْجِبَالِ فَأَبَيْنَ أَن يَحْمِلْنَهَا وَأَشْفَقْنَ مِنْهَا وَحَمَلَهَا الْإِنسَنُ إِنَّهُ كَانَ ظَلُومًا جَهُولًا

Indeed, we offered the Trust to the heavens and the earth and the mountains, and they declined to bear it and feared it; but man [undertook to] bear it. Indeed, he was unjust and ignorant.

Amanah (trust) means being responsible for following the rules and teachings of Shari'ah (Islamic law) and being required to obey them. If you do your best to follow these rules, you are promised the eternal rewards of Jannah (Paradise). But if you fail or disobey, you may face the punishment of Jahannam (Hell). It was said that Allah Ta'ala placed this amanah (trust) before the heavens, the earth, and the mountains and all of them refused to bear the burden of this responsibility shrinking from it out of the danger of not being able to fulfill its due right - but, man did. Some early commentators have considered this a figure of speech - as the noble Qur'an has said elsewhere by comparison.

Surah Al-Hashr 559:21

لَوْ أَنزَلْنَا هَٰذَا الْقُرْءَانَ عَلَىٰ جَبَلٍ لَّرَأَيْتَهُ خَٰشِعًا مُّتَصَدِّعًا مِّنْ خَشْيَةِ اللَّهِ وَتِلْكَ و
الْأَمْثَٰلُ نَضْرِبُهَا لِلنَّاسِ لَعَلَّهُمْ يَتَفَكَّرُونَ

If We had sent down this Qur'an upon a mountain, you would have seen it humbled and coming apart from fear of Allah. And these examples We present to the people that perhaps they will give thought.

It is obvious that this example has been given as a matter of supposition - not that it was really revealed to or on a mountain. So, these commentators have taken the 'offer' of 'trust' to the heavens, etc. also in a figurative or metaphorical sense. Allah knows the best.

In the verse, the words "Zalum" and "Jahul" refer to those people who did not follow the rules of Shari'ah as they should have and failed to fulfill the trust given to them. This includes disbelievers, hypocrites, wrongdoers, and sinning Muslims. This explanation comes from scholars like Sayyidna Ibn 'Abbas, Sayyidna Ibn Jubayr, Hasan Al-Basri, and others. (Qurtubi)

When we all agreed to come to earth, undergo this test, and then seek our place in heaven. Now Iblees is asking permission to allow him to live till the Day of Judgment. Allah allowed him.

Surah Al-Araf 7:15

قَالَ إِنَّكَ مِنَ الْمُنظَرِينَ

(Allah) said: "You are of those respited." (15)

Surah Al-Araf 7:16

قَالَ فَبِمَا أَغْوَيْتَنِي لَأَقْعُدَنَّ لَهُمْ صِرَاطَكَ الْمُسْتَقِيمَ

(Iblîs) said: "Because You have sent me astray, surely I will sit in wait against them (human beings) on Your Straight Path.

He said, "Because You made me slip, I will lie in wait for them on Your straight path." This means Allah has informed us that while there will be many paths if we remain steadfast on the straight path, we will return to our homes in heaven, which have already been created for us. However, Iblis has declared that he will be there to divert us from this straight path.

Surah Al-Araf 7:17

ثُمَّ لَآتِيَنَّهُم مِّنْ بَيْنِ أَيْدِيهِمْ وَمِنْ خَلْفِهِمْ وَعَنْ أَيْمَنِهِمْ وَعَن شَمَاءِلِهِمْ وَلَا تَجِدُ أَكْثَرَهُمْ شَكِرِينَ

Then I will come to them from before them and from behind them and on their right and on their left, and You will not find most of them grateful [to You]."

Some scholars interpret Iblees' influence from different directions metaphorically:

- From the front: Iblees distract you from moving towards Allah by convincing you that you have plenty of time and can prioritize worldly matters over spiritual duties.
- From the back: He prevents you from remembering the history of Islam and your purpose of creation. Some interpretations suggest this means reminding you of your past

indulgences and bad company when you try to turn towards Allah.

- From the left side: When you commit minor sins, he downplays their significance, making you believe they are trivial and leading you to continue doing wrong.
- From the right side: When you perform good deeds, he instills pride in you, making you think others are ignorant and that you are the most pious person. By attacking from all these directions, Iblees aims to lead you away from the path of Allah.

Ibless also said you will find most of them ungrateful.

Surah Al-Araf 7:18

[Allah] said, "Get out of Paradise, reproached and expelled. Whoever follows you among them I will surely fill Hell with you, all together."

Surah Al-Araf 7:19

وَيَادَمُ اسْكُنْ أَنتَ وَزَوْجُكَ الْجَنَّةَ فَكُلَا مِنْ حَيْثُ شِئْتُمَا وَلَا تَقْرَبَا هَذِهِ الشَّجَرَةَ فَتَكُونَا مِنَ الظَّلِمِينَ

And O Adam عَلَيْهِ السَّلَام dwell, you and your wife, in Paradise and eat from wherever you will but do not approach this tree, lest you be among the wrongdoers."

Here, the question arises, how was Hawa created?

Adam عَلَيْهِ السَّلَام desired companionship amidst the angels in paradise, and Allah granted his wish by presenting women as a precious gift to mankind. Allah instructed Adam عَلَيْهِ السَّلَام and Hawa to reside in Jannah.

Heaven is incomplete without a spouse. Marriage is often compared to Heaven, as it brings peace, love, and care. When you love, you care, but peace is essential to maintain these emotions. Sarcasm, harsh words, lying, insulting, and dishonesty disrupt peace, causing love and care to falter. Peace is not an emotion, but a state that sustains the feelings of love and care. While love and care fluctuate, having peace ensures their presence.

Here in Quran Allah says يَادَمُ ---Uskun -means sakeena

Spouse is peaceful but Ibless does not want us to be in peace so he tries very hard to break marriages and makes easy haram relationship.

Surah An-Nisa 4:1

يَأَيُّهَا النَّاسُ اتَّقُوا رَبَّكُمُ الَّذِي خَلَقَكُم مِّن نَّفْسٍ وَأَحِدَةٍ وَخَلَقَ مِنْهَا زَوْجَهَا وَبَثَّ مِنْهُمَا رِجَالًا كَثِيرًا وَنِسَاءً

O mankind, fear your Lord, who created you from one soul and created from it its mate and dispersed from both of them many men and women.

Many scholars understood this to mean that Allah Most High first created Adam عَلَيْهِ السَّلَام , and then from him, i.e., from his rib, our mother Hawa' (upon whom be peace) was created.

Hadith Sahi Bukhari

Narrated Abu Huraira: The Prophet (ﷺ) said, "Whoever believes in Allah and the Last Day should not hurt (trouble) his neighbor. And I advise you to take care of the women, for they are created from a rib and the most crooked portion of the rib is its upper part; if you try to straighten it, it will break, and if you leave it, it will remain crooked, so I urge you to take care of the women."

Allah moves Adam عَلَيْهِ السَّلَام and Hawa to paradise. And He tells them -

Surah Ta-Ha Aayah 20: 117-119

فَقُلْنَا يَادَمُ إِنَّ هَذَا عَدُوٌّ لَّكَ وَلِزَوْجِكَ فَلَا يُخْرِجَنَّكُمَا مِنَ الْجَنَّةِ فَتَشْقَىٰ (١١٧) إِنَّ لَكَ أَلَّا تَجُوعَ فِيهَا وَلَا تَعْرَى (١١٨) وَأَنَّكَ لَا تَظْمَؤُا فِيهَا وَلَا تَضْحَىٰ

Then We said: "O Adam عَلَيْهِ السَّلَام Verily, this is an enemy to you and to your wife. So let him not get you both out of Paradise, so that you will be distressed. (117) Verily, you have (a promise from Us) that you will never be hungry therein nor naked. (118) And you (will) suffer not from thirst therein nor from the sun's heat. (119)

(Surah Al-Baqarah, Quran 2:35)

وَقُلْنَا يَادَمُ اسْكُنْ أَنتَ وَزَوْجُكَ الْجَنَّةَ وَكُلَا مِنْهَا رَغَدًا حَيْثُ شِئْتُمَا وَلَا تَقْرَبَا هَذِهِ الشَّجَرَةَ فَتَكُونَا مِنَ الظَّلِمِينَ

And We said: "O Adam عَلَيْهِ السَّلَام Dwell you and your wife in the Paradise and eat both of you freely with pleasure and delight, of things therein as wherever you will, but come not near this tree or you both will be of the Zâlimûn (wrong-doers)." (35)

Allah said that if you go near the tree, you will be like those who do wrong (referring to Iblees, who had done wrong before). There was only one prohibition: do not go near the tree. Allah did not say "do not eat from the tree" but "do not go near the tree."

Iblees whispered to Adam عَلَيْهِ السَّلَام to approach the tree. Iblees can whisper to people and will continue to do so until the Day of Judgment. He did not tell them to go directly to the tree but to move gradually closer, step by step because the devil will whisper that it is not haram until you eventually commit a haram act.

Waswasa refers to the devil's whispers, which then disappear, making you think it is your idea.

Surah Al-Araf 7:20

فَوَسْوَسَ لَهُمَا الشَّيْطَانُ لِيُبْدِيَ لَهُمَا مَا وُ رِئَ عَنْهُمَا مِن سَوْءَاتِهِمَا وَقَالَ مَا نَهَىٰكُمَا رَبُّكُمَا عَنْ هَٰذِهِ الشَّجَرَةِ إِلَّا أَن تَكُونَا مَلَكَيْنِ أَوْ تَكُونَا مِنَ الْخَٰلِدِينَ

"But Satan whispered to them to make apparent to them that which was concealed from them of their private parts. He said, "Your Lord did not forbid you this tree except that you become angels or immortal."

Surah Ta-Ha 20: 120

إِلَيْهِ الشَّيْطَٰنُ قَالَ يَٰادَمُ هَلْ أَدُلُّكَ عَلَىٰ شَجَرَةِ الْخُلْدِ وَمُلْكٍ لَّا يَبْلَىٰ

Then Shaitân (Satan) whispered to him, saying: " Adam عَلَيْهِ السلام Shall I lead you to the Tree of Eternity and to a kingdom that will never waste away?"

Surah Al-Araf 7:21

وَقَاسَمَهُمَا إِنِّي لَكُمَا لَمِنَ النَّاصِحِينَ

And he swore [by Allah] to them, "Indeed, I am to you from among the sincere advisors."

Iblees deceived them by first saying that if they ate from the tree, they would become angels and live in heaven forever. We must remember that we were all created for earth, while our true homes were created in heaven. To enter paradise, we must pass the test, perform good deeds on earth, and then go to paradise. Iblees reminded Adam عَلَيْهِ السَّلَامُ that he is in heaven temporarily and was made khalifas for the earth. Iblees suggested that by eating from the tree, they could stay in heaven forever and become like angels. Adam عَلَيْهِ السَّلَامُ forgot that Allah had already honored human beings by creating them and making the angels bow down to Adam عَلَيْهِ السَّلَامُ

Surah Al-Baqara 2: 36

فَأَزَلَّهُمَا الشَّيْطَانُ عَنْهَا فَأَخْرَجَهُمَا مِمَّا كَانَا فِيهِ وَقُلْنَا اهْبِطُوا بَعْضُكُمْ لِبَعْضٍ عَدُوٌّ وَلَكُمْ فِي الْأَرْضِ مُسْتَقَرٌّ وَمَتَاعٌ إِلَىٰ حِينٍ

But Satan caused them to slip out of it and removed them from that [condition] in which they had been. And We said, "Go down, [all of you], as enemies to one another, and you will have upon the earth a place of settlement and provision for a time."

As they tasted the fruit, their clothes were removed.

The need to cover oneself is an essential aspect of human nature. Unlike animals, Allah did not provide humans with natural coverings but inspired them the urge to cover themselves. A person's clothing should reflect piety, meaning it should adequately conceal the body. It should neither be too shabby and cheap nor excessively expensive and extravagant relative to one's financial standing. Moreover, clothing should not lead to feelings of pride.

Surah Al-Araf 7:22

فَدَلَّىٰهُمَا بِغُرُورٍ فَلَمَّا ذَاقَا الشَّجَرَةَ بَدَتْ لَهُمَا سَوْءَٰتُهُمَا وَطَفِقَا يَخْصِفَانِ عَلَيْهِمَا مِن وَرَقِ الْجَنَّةِ وَنَادَىٰهُمَا رَبُّهُمَا أَلَمْ أَنْهَكُمَا عَن تِلْكُمَا الشَّجَرَةِ وَأَقُل لَّكُمَا إِنَّ الشَّيْطَٰنَ لَكُمَا عَدُوٌّ مُّبِينٌ

So he made them fall, through deception. And when they tasted of the tree, their private parts became apparent to them, and they began to fasten together over themselves from the leaves of Paradise. And their Lord called to them, "Did I not forbid you from that tree and tell you that Satan is to you a clear enemy?"

As they tasted the fruit, their clothes were removed, and they began covering themselves with the leaves of heaven. It is in human nature to cover oneself, as it brings dignity. Satan, however, wants us to be like animals, without clothes, and to expose our skin.

Then Allah called to them and said, "Did I not tell you that Satan would come at you from all sides and lead you astray? And did I not tell you not to eat from this tree?"

Surah Al-Araf 7:23

قَالَا رَبَّنَا ظَلَمْنَا أَنفُسَنَا وَإِن لَّمْ تَغْفِرْ لَنَا وَتَرْحَمْنَا لَنَكُونَنَّ مِنَ الْخَاسِرِينَ

They said, "Our Lord, we have wronged ourselves, and if You do not forgive us and have mercy upon us, we will surely be among the losers."

The lesson from this ayah is that if we make mistakes, we should turn to Allah's words and remind ourselves of His guidance.

Allah forgave them and told them to go to earth and for you, the earth is a place of settlement and enjoyment for a time.

Surah Al-Araf 7:26

يَٰبَنِي ءَادَمَ قَدْ أَنزَلْنَا عَلَيْكُمْ لِبَاسًا يُوَارِي سَوْءَٰتِكُمْ وَرِيشًا وَلِبَاسُ التَّقْوَىٰ ذَٰلِكَ خَيْرٌ
ذَٰلِكَ مِنْ ءَايَٰتِ اللَّهِ لَعَلَّهُمْ يَذَّكَّرُونَ

O children of Adam عَلَيْهِ السَّلَام *have bestowed upon you clothing to conceal your private parts and as adornment. But the clothing of righteousness that is best. That is from the signs of Allah that perhaps they will remember.*

Surah Al-Araf 7:27

يَبَنِي ءَادَمَ لَا يَفْتِنَنَّكُمُ الشَّيْطَنُ كَمَا أَخْرَجَ أَبَوَيْكُم مِّنَ الْجَنَّةِ يَنزِعُ عَنْهُمَا لِبَاسَهُمَا لِيُرِيَهُمَا سَوْءَاتِهِمَا إِنَّهُ يَرَنكُمْ هُوَ وَقَبِيلُهُ مِنْ حَيْثُ لَا تَرَوْنَهُمْ إِنَّا جَعَلْنَا الشَّيَاطِينَ أَوْلِيَاءَ لِلَّذِينَ لَا يُؤْمِنُونَ

O children of Adam عَلَيْهِ السَّلَام *not Satan tempt you as he removed your parents from Paradise, stripping them of their clothing to show them their private parts. Indeed, he sees you, he and his tribe, from where you do not see them. Indeed, We have made the devil allies to those who do not believe.*

Surah Al-Mumenoon 23:97

وَقُل رَّبِّ أَعُوذُ بِكَ مِنْ هَمَزَاتِ الشَّيَاطِينِ (٩٧) وَأَعُوذُ بِكَ رَبِّ أَن يَحْضُرُونِ

And say, "My Lord, I seek refuge in You from the incitements of the devils,

Surah Al-Mumenoon 23: 98

وَأَعُوذُ بِكَ رَبِّ أَن يَحْضُرُونِ (٩٨) حَتَّىٰ إِذَا جَاءَ أَحَدَهُمُ الْمَوْتُ قَالَ رَبِّ ارْجِعُونِ

And I seek refuge in You, my Lord, lest they be present with me."

Allah has taught us how to protect ourselves from Shaitan's schemes. Shaitan's influence will be greatly weakened by following Allah's Book and reciting Surah Al-Falaq and Surah An-Naas.

Surah Al-Araf 7:24

قَالَ اهْبِطُوا بَعْضُكُمْ لِبَعْضٍ عَدُوٌّ وَلَكُمْ فِي الْأَرْضِ مُسْتَقَرٌّ وَمَتَعٌ إِلَىٰ حِينٍ

[Allah] said, "Descend, being to one another enemies. And for you on the earth is a place of settlement and enjoyment for a time."

"Enemies to each other" means failing to remind one another of Allah's words. For example, if a man is doing wrong and his wife does not remind him of Allah, he will continue his wrongdoing. Similarly, if he earns money through haram means for his family, it means his family becomes his enemy. Only by reminding each other of Allah can we save ourselves; otherwise, we become enemies to one another.

He added, "There you will live, there you will die, and from there you will be resurrected."

Surah Al-Araf 7:25

قَالَ فِيهَا تَحْيَوْنَ وَفِيهَا تَمُوتُونَ وَمِنْهَا تُخْرَجُونَ

He said, "Therein you will live, and therein you will die, and from it you will be brought forth."

Shaytan deceived Adam عَلَيْهِ السَّلَام and Hawā. Allah says. They made a mistake and they ate from the tree.

What is the difference between Shaytan's mistake and Adam عَلَيْهِ السلام mistake

Shaytan was unrepentant, whereas Adam عَلَيْهِ السَّلَام and Hawa were repentant.

Then Adam عَلَيْهِ السَّلَام received from his Lord [some] words, and He accepted his repentance.

Surah Al-Baqarah, Quran 2:37

فَتَلَقَّى ءَادَمُ مِن رَّبِّهِ كَلِمَةٍ فَتَابَ عَلَيْهِ إِنَّهُ هُوَ التَّوَّابُ الرَّحِيمُ

Then Adam عَلَيْهِ السَّلَام *received from his Lord Words. And his Lord pardoned him (accepted his repentance). Verily, He is the One Who forgives (accepts repentance), the Most Merciful.*

That's where knowledge comes into play again. Allah taught Adam عَلَيْهِ السَّلَام the words of repentance. Adam عَلَيْهِ السَّلَام learned from his mistakes. And then Allah says

Surah Al-Baqara 2: 38

قُلْنَا اهْبِطُواْ مِنْهَا جَمِيعًا فَإِمَّا يَأْتِيَنَّكُم مِّنِّى هُدًى فَمَن تَبِعَ هُدَايَ فَلَا خَوْفٌ عَلَيْهِمْ وَلَا هُمْ يَحْزَنُونَ) ٣٨(

We said: "Get down all of you from this place (the Paradise), then whenever there comes to you Guidance from Me, and whoever follows My Guidance, there shall be no fear on them, nor shall they grieve.

From this, we learn that if we adhere to the Book of Allah, the Quran, we will not experience fear or sadness. These two states are reserved for paradise, where there is no fear or grief. However, by following the Quran, our life on earth can resemble a life in paradise. May Allah help us to read and follow His Book QURAN.

Surah Al-Baqara 2:39

وَالَّذِينَ كَفَرُوا وَكَذَّبُوا بِايَتِنَا أُوْلَبِكَ أَصْحَبُ النَّارِ هُمْ فِيهَا خَالِدُونَ

But those who disbelieve and belie Our Ayât (proofs, evidence, verses, lessons, signs, revelations, etc.)- such are the dwellers of the Fire, They shall abide therein forever. whoever follows My Guidance, there shall be no fear on them, nor shall they grieve.

Those who do not believe in this message have befriended devils, happily discarding their clothes and disregarding the distinctions between halal and haram. They become companions of Satan in this world.

Ready to descend to earth

Adam عَلَيْهِ السَّلَام was ready to descend to earth after those three things happened:

Allah showed that Adam عَلَيْهِ السَّلَام can learn

Adam عَلَيْهِ السَّلَام made a mistake

Adam عَلَيْهِ السَّلَام learned from that mistake and sought repentance.

Once those three things were complete, "Now go to the earth. Now, descend to the earth."

Surah Al-Baqarah, Quran 2:36

On earth will be a dwelling place for you and an enjoyment for a time."

And on this earth, you have a place to reside and you have some provision, for a small amount of time, for a temporary existence. Allah did not say, "There you will be tortured and there you will be punished and there you will suffer." He said, "This is a place for you to reside and your provision for a time and that time will end. That time is temporary." So the plan was to send Adam عَلَيْهِ السَّلَام and Hawa to earth This distinction between the angels, Iblees, and Adam عَلَيْهِ السَّلَام is crucial. Angels lack free will and the ability to learn. Adam عَلَيْهِ السَّلَام on the other hand, possesses free will and the capacity to learn from mistakes, repenting when necessary. Iblees, despite having free will, chose to use it for evil, displaying rebellion, arrogance, and an absence of repentance.

We are the descendants of Adam عَلَيْهِ السَّلَام. Like him, we are meant to learn from our mistakes, seek forgiveness from Allah, and grow spiritually. We pray to Allah for guidance and assistance in this journey.

Author's Note

I have written The Concept of Khalifa | Unveiling the Meaning and Majesty Volume 1 as my first book. May this book bring you valuable insights and growth. Jazakallahu Khairan for taking the time to read it. I ask you to please pray for me, as I will do the same for you. As-salamu alaykum.

-Farhat

9 789363 039551

Printed at Repro India Ltd.